IMAGES OF ENGLAND

SALTBURN-
BY–THE–SEA
REVISITED

IMAGES OF ENGLAND

SALTBURN-BY-THE-SEA
REVISITED

CATH AND TONY LYNN

The History Press

Frontispiece: Saltburn Water Tower was located on the corner of Upleatham and Lune Streets; water was pumped from Skelton Beck and stored in a large tank in the upper part of the structure. It was the main source of water for the town until water was brought from Lockwood Beck reservoir. It was erected by the North Eastern Railway Company in 1865 and demolished in 1905. It was home to several families of railway workers including the Donaldson family who occupied part of it for over thirty years.

First published in 2006 by Tempus Publishing

Reprinted in 2012 by
The History Press
The Mill, Brimscombe Port,
Stroud, Gloucestershire, GL5 2QG
www.thehistorypress.co.uk

British Library Cataloguing in Publication Data.
A catalogue record for this book is available from the British Library.

ISBN 978 0 7524 3773 6

Typesetting and origination by
Tempus Publishing Limited.
Printed in Great Britain.

Contents

	Acknowledgements	6
	Introduction	7
one	Buildings and Streets	9
two	Businesses and Shops	19
three	Sports and Events	31
four	Schools and Youth	39
five	Railways	55
six	People	67
seven	The Pier and Cliff Lift	97
eight	By the Sea	111

Acknowledgements

The authors appreciate the valuable help given to them by many people during the years it has taken to accumulate and research the information and photographs. Thanks must also go to the staff of our local Archives at Middlesbrough and Northallerton who have been very helpful on our many visits and our own local library and Tourist Information Office who refer enquiring visitors to us, contact which often results in further information for us too.

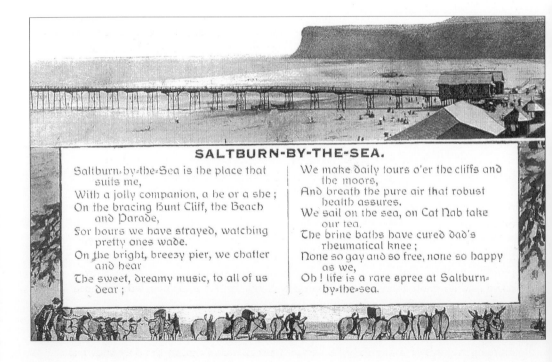

SALTBURN-BY-THE-SEA.

Saltburn-by-the-Sea is the place that suits me,
With a jolly companion, a he or a she;
On the bracing Hunt Cliff, the Beach and Parade,
For hours we have strayed, watching pretty ones wade.
On the bright, breezy pier, we chatter and hear
The sweet, dreamy music, to all of us dear;

We make daily tours o'er the cliffs and the moors,
And breath the pure air that robust health assures.
We sail on the sea, on Cat Nab take our tea.
The brine baths have cured dad's rheumatical knee;
None so gay and so free, none so happy as we,
Oh! life is a rare spree at Saltburn-by-the-sea.

Introduction

On the North Yorkshire coast there was a small hamlet called Saltburn in the parish of
Brotton; the hamlet was near the outflow from Skelton Beck into the sea. Saltburn is
first mentioned in the Register of Whitby Abbey as being the site of a hermitage given
to Whitby about the year 1215, by Roger de Argentum, who showed a taste for secluded
beauty so generally possessed by his monkish brethren.

Old Saltburn originally consisted of about a score of houses, some of decent
pretensions, built of dressed stone, the rest being more humble dwellings, usually
inhabited by the simple fishermen. Several of the houses were demolished on the decline
of the smuggling trade, for which the place was notorious in days gone by, leaving but
a single row of half a dozen cottages at the foot of Cat Nab and only a few feet above
the high-water mark. Two or three detached dwellings and a watermill behind Cat
Nab complete Old Saltburn. Small as the hamlet was, it boasted of at least three public
houses. The Ship Inn was the most notorious, especially when kept by John Andrews,
one of the most infamous smugglers of the period.

Alum works existed in the neighbourhood from about 1680 to 1720 and alum
manufacture was revived in 1765 by John Hall Stevenson Esq., of Skelton Castle,
and continued for a few years before it was finally abandoned. Some small trading
was carried on by means of luggers (small flat-bottomed sailing ships) capable of
being beached, for the purpose of loading and unloading. Lime, limestone and coal
were the principal imports and oak timber, pit props, alum, corn and hazel rods for
the manufacture of the corves (a form of shallow basket) used in the coal pits were
exported.

The smuggling system became so notorious that a detachment of coastguards were
stationed at the Blue House above the village of Saltburn. The decline of smuggling
probably resulted from the diminishing returns in addition to increased vigilance by
coastguards. A quote from a Saltburn guide is as follows: 'Since the merry days alluded
to, the glory of old Saltburn has departed – its smuggling days passed away – its gin
vaults have disappeared – and the gay roisterers, who were won't to make Cat Nab and
the adjacent rocks resound with their orgies, now lie beneath the green hillocks in the
retired graveyards of Brotton and Skelton'. Thenceforward, Saltburn was only known as
one of the adjuncts of Redcar; and occasional picnics were held at the place to drink tea
and eat 'fat rascals' (a type of scone) for which the Ship Inn was famous.

Land to the west of Skelton Beck was owned by Lord Zetland and farmed by a tenant at Rifts House Farm. The use of this land was to change dramatically when Royal Assent for an Act of Parliament was granted to extend the Stockton & Darlington Railway Company line from Redcar to Saltburn. Henry Pease, a member of a Quaker family, formed the Saltburn Improvement Company with the intention of building a new seaside resort on the fields of Rifts House Farm. The first foundation stone for the new town was laid on 23 January 1861 for a terrace to be named Alpha Place, this was the beginning of Saltburn-by-the-Sea as we know it today. Opening of the railway station to passenger traffic took place on 17 August 1861 and the opening of the pleasure grounds, now known as Valley Gardens, occurred at the end of 1861 and early in 1862 a charge was made for entry to the grounds. A boy christened Arthur Spencer was the first child born in the new town, on 1 June 1862, and he was the son of a stonemason. The Zetland Hotel was completed and opened by the railway company on 27 July 1863.

Visitors began arriving to Saltburn in increasing numbers but many found the steep paths to the beach tiresome and difficult. This problem was resolved by the construction of a timber vertical hoist later replaced by the famous water-balanced cliff lift.

The town has changed over the years; many of the old building have been adapted to meet modern requirements and some cherished buildings demolished. It is interesting to note that the early Victorian road system, designed to cater for the horse and cart age, coped better with the ever-growing demands placed by the motor car than many of today's modern estates.

Cath came to Saltburn at an early age and acquired valuable memories of life and the people of the town through her mother, who worked for over fifty years in Hamilton's Library in Milton Street. The earliest memories of Saltburn for Tony, who was born in Guisborough, are Sunday school day trips to the town, arriving always by train and having the most enjoyable times on the fine sandy beach and paddling in the cold North Sea. After their marriage in 1955 they made their home in the town, becoming involved in many activities, photographing people and attending events throughout the years. The town is still linked to the national railway system and thanks to our Victorian forebears is much used at the present time.

Despite the ups and downs of the town's existence its population has always managed to come out smiling and is always a splendid community to be part of.

Cath and Tony Lynn
May 2006

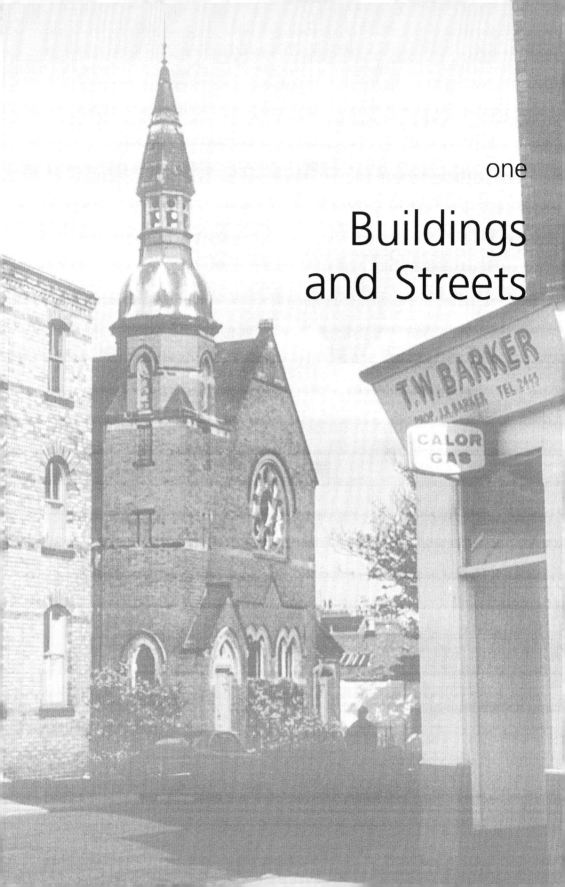

one

Buildings
and Streets

Architect Thomas Oliver from Newcastle-upon-Tyne designed Saltburn Convalescent Home. Financed by Joseph Pease at a cost of £12,000 it was opened in 1872 and provided convalescent accommodation for workers from around the area. In September 1904 Silcoates private school used it as a temporary base while their fire-damaged premises in Wakefield were rebuilt.

Saltburn Convalescent Home was purchased by the Workingmen's Club and Institute Union for £6,000 and continued as a convalescent home after a £2,000 refurbishment. It was re-opened on 11 September 1909 by the Rt Hon. Herbert Samuel MP. We believe this photograph was taken at that re-opening. During the Second World War following bomb damage to the Saltburn Council School in Upleatham Street, pupils were taught on the premises from 1941 to 1943. It is still in use as a convalescent and holiday home.

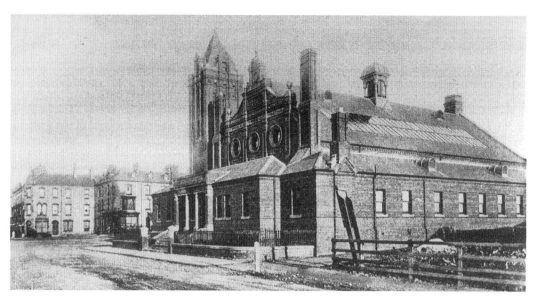

The Swimming Baths were opened officially by Arthur Pease Esq. on Monday 11 May 1891. The frontage faced the railway station and the swimming pool was in the centre of the building. The pool was filled with seawater pumped from an inlet offshore near to the pier. Other facilities on offer included private brine, needle, douche and electric baths. Massage facilities were also available.

The swimming pool in use by girls from The Towers private school. The seawater in the pool was changed once a week. The water was officially described as 'tepid' but from personal experience we would say it was cold. Demolition of the baths took place in July 1976 by Blair & Co. of Stockton.

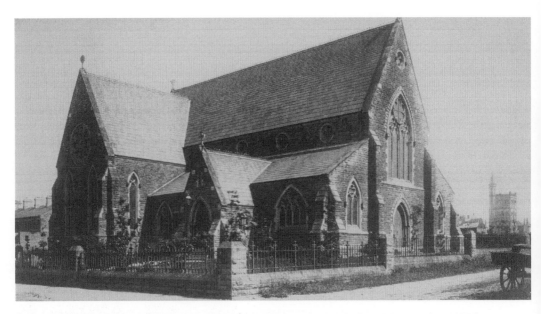

Emmanuel parish church on Windsor Road. The foundation stone was laid on 29 September 1867 by the Earl of Zetland and the church opened for worship on 4 August 1868 and was consecrated on 31 July 1872 by the Bishop of York. The Revd Benjamin Irvin was the first vicar of the parish and served for a total of forty years.

Emmanuel parish church. An initial gift of £1,000 by the Marquess of Zetland and further subscriptions enabled a tower to be erected at the west end of the church and a peal of eight bells was provided by Mr A.J. Dorman JP. The Queen Victoria memorial clock was added by public subscription and the foundation stone for the tower was laid on 7 August 1900. Dedication of the bells, by the Lord Bishop of Beverley, took place on 9 June 1902.

Above: Albion Terrace Primitive Methodist church foundation stone was laid 12 April 1909 and the church dedicated in April 1910. The last service was held on 28 September 1969. Fortunately the planned demolition did not take place and the building was bought by Saltburn & Marske UDC to be rented to the Towns Community Association at a peppercorn rent. It is now used as a community centre and theatre.

Right: The Congregational church in Pearl Street. The foundation stone was laid in October 1892 and the church opened on 8 July 1893. Its first service was held on Sunday 9 July 1893 and it closed on 29 December 1971. Demolition followed very quickly and Hanover House was built on the site of the church and the adjacent Cromwell Hall.

Glenhow School, Albion Terrace. The building was formerly two houses and became a private school for boys in around 1884. It returned to private occupation in 1893 until 1901. It is unclear exactly when it became Glenhow School. It finally closed in 1992 at which time girls were also being educated in the school. Princess Anne visited the school on 21 February 1986 and it has now been converted into town houses.

It was originally intended that the Assembly Rooms be erected on the corner of Milton Street and Britannia Terrace however, lack of funding prevented this. In 1884 Assembly Rooms to a different design were built part-way down 'Cart Bank' and became known as the Spa Pavilion catering for many events, including dances, school presentations, ice and roller skating. It is now the Spa Hotel providing meals and hotel accommodation for visitors.

Red Lodge, Marine Parade. These properties were built in 1872 and command fine sea views. The centre property is the Masonic Hall. The basement, much strengthened, served as the ARP headquarters during the Second World War. Dr Burnett lived on the left-hand side of the property with the surgery at the rear. It is now the Marine Hotel.

Above left: A Red Lodge Pension advertisement placed in a Saltburn brochure of around 1909. This was the property on the right-hand side and it was used for many years by Saltburn High School for Girls.

Above right: No. 5 Zetland Terrace. The terrace was built on an area which was the site of Rifts House Farm owned by Zetland Estates whose adjacent land was originally chosen for the building of the resort of Saltburn-by-the-Sea. Lucy Whiteley is on the doorstep.

Marske Mill in the Riftswood Valley. Water was drawn from Skelton Beck to power the waterwheel. It was not used commercially as a mill after the 1920s but continued in use as a small farmstead. It was finally demolished in 1972 although evidence of its existence is still visible. The building on the right-hand side is believed to be for the engineer in charge of building the nearby viaduct.

Marske Mill viewed from the railway viaduct just prior to demolition. A full archaeological survey was made of the site and a report published of its findings. The concrete weir further upstream on Skelton Beck is still in position.

Eden Street, north side. These houses were built by the North Eastern Railway Company as homes for their employees and was known when built as Railway Terrace.

Eden Street, south side. The first property in the terrace was originally a corner shop that eventually became a doctor's surgery. It is now a private residence.

Station Street. Looking north from the Community Centre tower. The Queen Hotel on the right-hand side opened in 1875 and the building on the left was purpose built as a post office and opened in 1901. All mail for East Cleveland was sorted here and the first floor housed the area's telephone exchange.

A view from the Emmanuel parish church tower looking towards Skelton in around 1965. Cambridge Street is in the foreground and Princes Road on the right.

two

Businesses
and Shops

RAPP AND SONS
BOOKSELLERS & STATIONERS 3
CIRCULATING LIBRARY
PIANOS ON SALE OR HIRE
LIBRARY

Above: The premises of D. Mazzetti, decorator, in Milton Street. This later became Gresty's Pet Stores, a second-hand car dealer's showroom, and is now Healthwise Fitness centre.

Right: Mazzetti's general dealers shop in Garnet Street. The premises were formerly occupied by Skelton Co-op which moved to new premises in Dundas Street West in 1929.

Opposite: Rapp & Sons' shop in Dundas Street East sold a wide range of goods, had a lending library and sold and rented pianos. They also published a weekly newspaper which in addition to local news contained the names of visitors, their hometowns and the hotel or boarding house where they were staying. William Rapp was postmaster from 1873 until his retirement in July 1894. The shop is now part of the Victoria Hotel.

Dundas Street East, *c.* 1909. The photograph shows fifteen small businesses between them selling a wide variety of goods. Compare the upper two floors with the photograph below; there has been little change over the years.

Dundas Street East, *c.* 1989. Don Hibbert began business in Upleatham Street at the corner of Cambridge Street and later moved to these larger premises selling television sets, radios, electrical goods and hardware. He opened further premises in Dundas Street carrying the Hibbert name and run by his two sons.

Station Square, c. 1905. The shops on the right were severely damaged during the Second World War and had to be demolished after a bomb dropped on an adjacent air-raid shelter. The site remained undeveloped for a number of years until a car showroom was built and opened by Keith Watson. It is currently Andrew Watson's furniture and carpet showroom.

Skelton Co-operative Society's purpose-built premises in Dundas Street West opened in 1929 and closed in 1996. The photograph was taken in 1996 prior to closure. It was used for a time as a second-hand car showroom before conversion to town houses.

Left: Provincial Building Society office in Milton Street. The beautiful wrought-iron balcony over the entrance door was removed shortly after the photograph was taken.

Below: Melliship's Stores Ltd in Milton Street, advertised in 1910 as the oldest established grocers, provision, wine and spirit stores in Saltburn-by-the-Sea. They were also noted as tea and coffee specialists. They also had a shop in Dundas Street. The Milton Street shop is now Keith's Sports.

Right: The premises of J.J. Wilson in Station Street. The young man standing outside is Tommy Wilson. The shop eventually became Furbanks the tobacconists. A very ornate shop frontage was lost when modernisation took place and it became Home Bakery, as can be seen below.

Below: Here are three businesses that served the town for many years in Station Street. The Token Shop owned by Maurice Downs offered an excellent service selling LP records and fancy goods. The rooms above Home Bakery were used as a dentist's surgery. Langmans chemist's was another shop that sold a wide range of goods besides a dispensing service for medicines.

Windsor Garage stood on the corner of Windsor Road and Princes Road and was owned by Percy Sanders. Next door was Ivanhoe Press owned by J. Parks. The site is now occupied by the car showroom of Watson Ford.

Saltburn Electric Laundry, Randolph Street with a driver, assistants and vans on display. The two vehicles on the left are different models of Morris Commercial vans. People in the photograph are, from left to right: R. Mossom, -?-, -?-, -?-, L. Dawe, ? Murdock, -?-, N. Rudham, -?-, E. Baker. An advertisement in the parish magazine for November 1900 claims that it was the first laundry in the kingdom where the machinery was driven by electric power.

De Bonne kitchen and bedroom showroom, Marske Road. This was originally Medd's bakery and garage. Afternoon teas were served upstairs and in fine weather on the terrace over the garage. The site still has a garage but the showrooms are now the Saltburn Artists Gallery and work units. Note the price of petrol, *c.* 1980.

Russell & Sanderson's removal van, a converted ex-army lorry, outside The Ridge, a Dr Barnardo's Home in Marske Mill Lane. The home closed in 1969. Ossie Russell is on the left-hand side of the trio. Ossie's removal business is now run by his son.

JOHN W. LIDDLE, D.B.O.A.

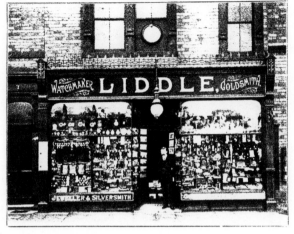

Above: Advertisement for Liddle's shop in Dundas Street East. The premises are now Hibbert's TV and electrical engineering shop.

Left: Advertisement for Mazzetti's shop in Dundas Street which is now Virgo's coffee shop.

Opposite below: Cosy Bingo and Social Club, Milton Street. The first building on this site was the Primitive Methodist church, built in 1866, and was later converted into a cinema by blacking out the windows. It was extended and became the Cosy Cinema. Closure of the Bingo and Social Club took place in November 1995 and demolition followed. The site is now a block of flats.

Above: Watson's car sales and garage in Milton Street. The shop was built in around 1866 and operated for many years as a high-class confectioners and caterers. It was the meeting place for the Saltburn Rotary Club. Watson's built and operated a garage next door and eventually used the premises as a car spares shop and store. Demolition of the property took place in January 2002. The site is now occupied by a block of flats.

King's shop in Station Street sold a wide range of goods, including newspapers, magazines, cigarettes, toys, Hornby Dublo railway models, leather goods, pictures, china. It was a very popular shop much missed when it closed on Thursday 30 June 2005. This is John King with two members of his staff, Hillary Mowbrey and Liz Banks.

King's of Saltburn, Station Street. These are the early morning girls who were for many years responsible for preparing the newspaper rounds for delivery and keeping the magazine stock up to date. Most importantly they greeted the early morning customers with a smile and banter. Kath Walker is on the left and Ann Butler on the right.

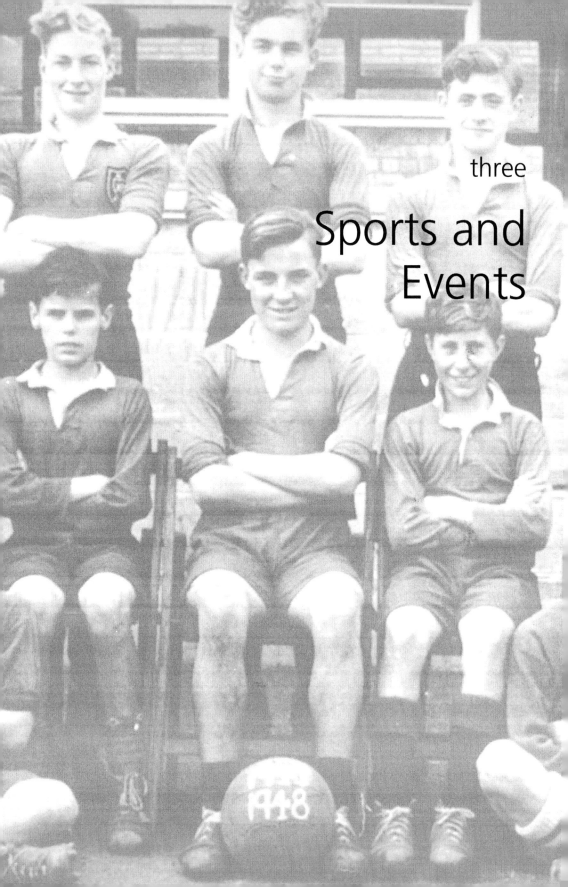

three

Sports and Events

Above: Grass tennis courts below the Halfpenny Bridge in the Valley Gardens, *c.* 1889. The bridge owned by Skelton Estates was built in 1869 and demolished in December 1974 when it became unsafe.

Left: Players on the grass tennis courts below Halfpenny Bridge in the Valley Gardens.

Opposite: A 'keep fit' evening class at the Saltburn High School for Girls, *c.* 1950. From left to right, back row: Margaret Constable, -?-, ? Earnshaw, -?-. Second row: Margaret Blair, ? Watson, -?-, -?-, -?-. Third row: Cathleen Naisbitt, Jean Hunter, Avis Featherstone, Hilda Witt, Mrs Tonkin (instructor). Front row: -?-, Margaret Ellerton, -?-.

Saltburn Cricket Club players in the first all-ladies match to be played in Saltburn, July 1946. Left to right, back row: Joyce Medd, -?-, ? Marwood-Smith, Freda Burns, ? Robertson, -?-, -?-, -?-, Jean Smith, -?-, Essie Waterton, Madge White. Middle row: Lottie Readman, -?-, ? Robertson, Barbara Chapman, Margaret Robinson, -?-, Maureen Chapman, Doreen Lines, ? Davidson. Front row: -?-, Dr Murray, Arnold Davidson.

Above: Saltburn Bowling Club members with the club flag. Left to right: Fred Hatfield, Charlie Southcote, -?-, -?-, -?-, Frank Hudson, -?-, Frank Ableson, -?-, -?-, ? Hildon, -?-, -?-, -?-, -?-, ? Dungay, -?-, Arthur Gladders, ? Taplin.

Opposite below: Saltburn High School for Girls hockey team.

Above: Saltburn hockey team, 1905. Games were often played on the beach and it was sometimes a race against the tide to complete the game. Left to right, back row: Tom Nelson, -?-, -?-, -?-, -?-, -?-, W. Horsley. Front row: -?-, -?-, -?-, Alan Hick, C. Copeland.

Saltburn hockey team at Bridlington, 1953. Left to right, back row: Bernard Pennock, Keith Archer, Redvers Blakey, Eric Sibley. Front row: Miles Atterton, -?-, T. Robinson, ? Pennock, Wilf Hearn.

Saltburn Victorian footballers. A group of enthusiastic amateur footballers who follow Victorian rules and wear Victorian dress in aid of charities.

A football team photographed near the tennis courts on Marske Mill Lane. Left to right, back row: J. Ford, Ron Hinchely, A. Fishburn, Reg Harkness, B. Coates, Front row: T. Harrison, L. Lowery, Charlie Darnborough, B. Kemball, E. Spencer, F. Atkinson.

Upleatham Street School football team, 1947/48. Left to right, back row: Fred Webster (headmaster), Jim Elliot, Ron Denham, Bruce Watson, Norman Fisher, Keith Calvert, George Bowman. Middle row: Peter Cole, John Robinson, John Suscens, John Flintoff, Peter Leonard. Front row: Doug Kirk and Dennis Turner.

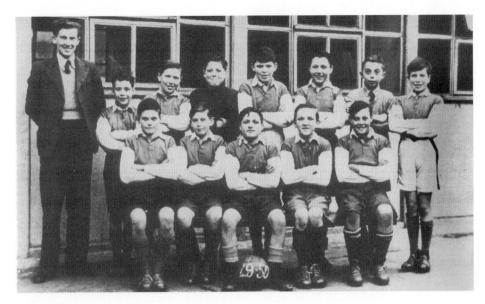

Upleatham Street County School football team, 1949/50. Teacher: Mr D. Harrison. Left to right, back row: -?-, David Cole, John Heath, Maurice Metcalfe, George Walshaw, Roger Lobley, Peter Smith. Front row: Brian Jones, Geoffrey Horner, Albert Robinson, Tommy Ward and Richard Healey.

Upleatham Street School Tug of War Team. Back row: Jim Elliott, Bruce Watson, John Boyes. Front row: Douglas Kirk, Norman Fisher, Ronnie Denham, John Suscens, Keith Calvert.

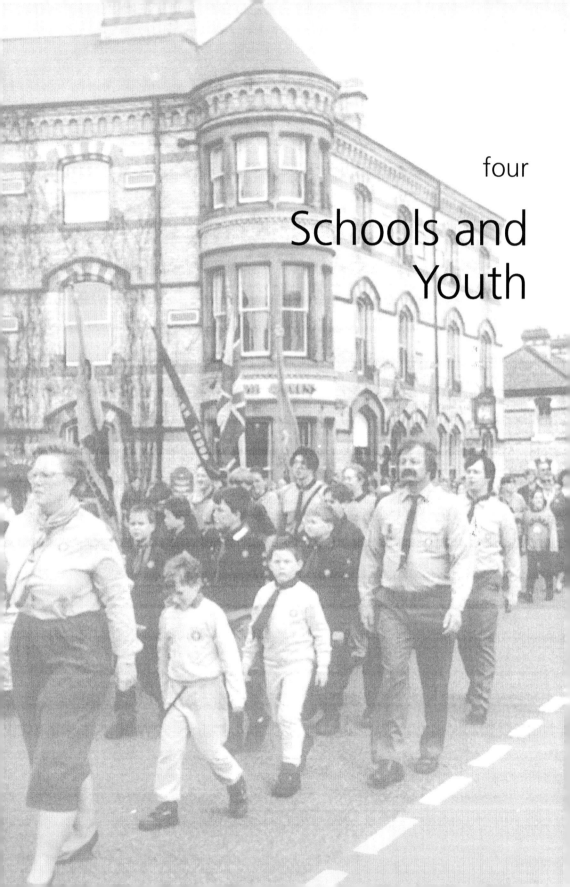

four

Schools and
Youth

The Towers was built as a private residence in 1881 and became the Towers School for Girls. The school expanded into adjacent properties in around 1917, a gymnasium was built and a tennis court provided on Windsor Road. In 1954 the school closed and was converted into flats.

The Towers School gymnasium.

The Towers School common room.

The Towers School bedroom.

First Saltburn Brownies outdoors at Hob Hill with District Commissioner Sue Sotheran.

First Saltburn Brownie pack holiday at Littlebeck, August 1966. Left to right, back row: Tawny Owl, Cathleen Lynn, Margaret Newman, -?-, -?-, Dorothy Newman, -?-. Second row: Pat Moody, Christine Anderson, -?-, -?-, Carol Sanderson, Jackie Hoskins, Third row: Christine Lyon, -?-, Carol Broadhurst, Ross Johnson, -?-, Front row: -?-, Jane Appleby-Brown, -?-, Jane Lynn, Janet Thornton, Margaret Nisbet, District Commissioner.

Guides and Brownies parade along Albion Terrace to the Cenotaph for a Remembrance Service, c. 1975.

Brownies and Cubs parade in Upleatham Street. Owen Banks is the Scout leader at the back and Brownie Guider, Marion Smith, carries a handbag.

Red Cross cadets in a Remembrance Parade on Sunday 13 November 1994.

Army cadets entering Somerfield car park during the Remembrance Parade in 1994.

The Church Lads Brigade band poses outside the Assembly Rooms, *c.* 1903.

The Church Lads Brigade band and cadets outside Emmanuel church. Left to right, back row: -?-, Elgey, the Revd Benjamin Irvin, Moutry, Holland, Poll. Second row: Moss, Bowers, -?-, -?-, -?-, -?-, Torringlar, -?-, P. Haw. Third row: -?-, J. Clark, Springet, Frank Bainbridge, A. Downs, Bates, Agnew, Evans, Clark. Front row: Hinchley, -?-, -?-, -?-, -?-, -?-, -?-, -?-.

The sixth form at an art lesson in Saltburn High School for Girls, *c.* 1952.

Above: A mixed choir from Glenhow School singing for the Britain in Bloom judges in Station Square, August 1991.

Opposite below: Saltburn Junior School pupils with headmaster John White.

Above: Saltburn County Infants School, Class 1, 1930. Left to right, back row: John Barber, Frank Hoggarth, Malcolm Ashforth, Dennis Straight, Gordon Hicks, Gordon Robinson, -?-, Peter Boyes, Arnold Burton, -?-, Basil Bird. Middle row: Kathleen Austin, Nita Burnett, Ann Coates, Sylvia Harland, Joyce Dungay, Freda Woodrow, Nora Gash, Barbara Stubbs, Marjorie Brown, Gwen Richardson. Front row: George Hinchley, Jean Burton, Nora Omerod, Jean Theaker, Betty Parkes, Edith Winterton, Jean Readman, Zena Robinson, Tommy Oxendale.

Saltburn County Infants reception class, 1950. The teacher standing is Miss Ogilvy and seated is Miss Watson.

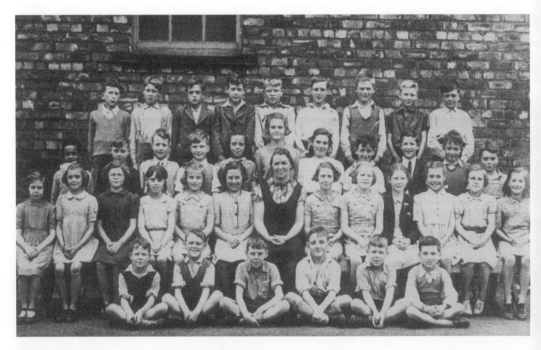

Saltburn Junior School with teacher Miss Harburn.

Saltburn Infant School class, c. 1964. Left to right, back row: Kathleen Boyes, Jane Appleby-Brown, -?-, Carol Sanderson, Margaret Phillips, -?-, Helen Burrel. Middle row: Carolyn Horn, -?-, Janet Thornton, Pauline Harrington, Jane Lynn. Front row: -?-, Susan Postlethwaite, Jackie Hoskins, Catherine Anderson.

Saltburn Junior School class, c. 1956.

Above: Saltburn Huntcliff School pupils after planting daffodil bulbs on Marske Mill Lane in Autumn 1994 accompanied by George Barnes.

Right: Saltburn Primary School children dressed in Victorian clothes to celebrate 110 years of the Cliff Lift on Tuesday 28 June 1994.

Opposite above: A visit by Cath and Tony Lynn to Saltburn Infants School to give an illustrated local history talk, *c.* 1990

Opposite below: Saltburn Huntcliff School. Pupils plant spring bulbs near the entrance to the school on Marske Mill Lane with Keith Ferry, Woodland Warden, *c.* 1997.

Saltburn Primary School children with Northumbrian water engineer Steve Coverdale after naming a tunnel–excavating machine to be used in the sewage disposal improvement scheme, *c.* 1995.

Saltburn Primary School children with Michael Bates MP at the painting of a mural on the chalets wall to celebrate the commissioning of the sewage pumping station on Friday 28 June 1996.

Saltburn Infants School, Upleatham Street, summer fête, 1991. Retained fireman, Tommy Paterson, gives a demonstration.

The treasure hunt stall at Saltburn Infants School summer fête, 1991. Headmistress Janet Richardson is on the right.

St George's Day Parade of Cubs, Scouts and Guides from East Cleveland along Windsor Road on Sunday 23 April 1995.

Cub, Scout and Guide standard bearers outside Emanuel church on St George's Day, 1995.

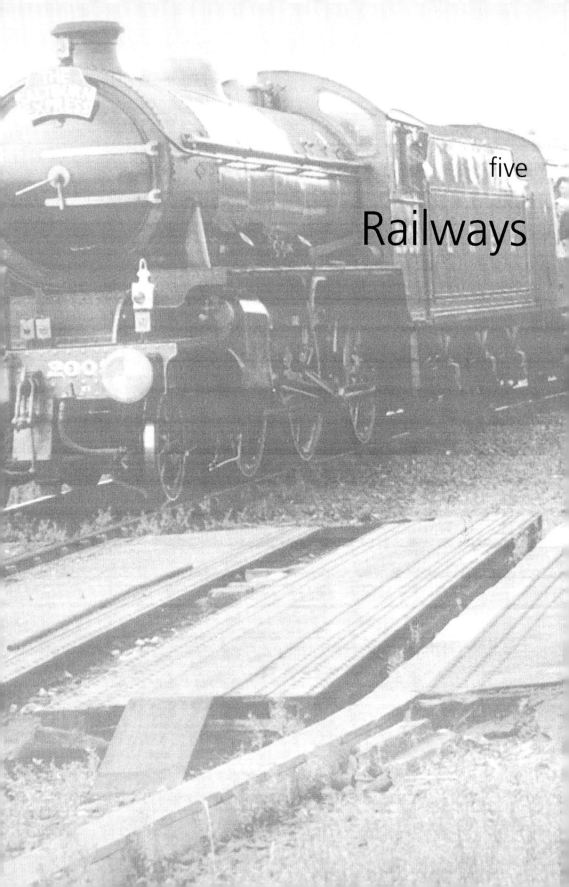

five

Railways

Above: Saltburn Riftswood viaduct shown here under construction. It was opened for mineral traffic 1 June 1872 and passenger traffic 1 April 1875. It is a brick structure with eleven elliptical arches, 783ft long and 150ft high at is highest point. To the credit of Victorian engineers and builders the viaduct is still carrying loads associated with steelmaking and mining.

Left: An Austerity locomotive crossing Saltburn Riftswood viaduct with a coal train. The scene was captured on film by Jack Claxton as his son Ian watched, entranced by the sight and sound of the locomotive hauling its load.

Above: Four locomotives, two LNER Class V.2 and two LMS Stanier 2-6-0, approaching Black Bridge after being turned on the Skelton Triangle, *c.* 1957. These locomotives brought excursion trains to Redcar and Saltburn and had to be turned before making the return journey. It was unusual to see four engines coupled together on this duty.

Right: Two locomotives, an Ivatt 2-6-0 and an LNER B1, in Jubilee sidings, Saltburn, waiting to turn on the Skelton Triangle after bringing Bank Holiday excursions to the town.

Replacement of the stone-arched railway bridge in progress on Windsor Road, August 1961. We remember leaving the town for a holiday at this time and passing under the stone-arched bridge on the way out and on our return, a fortnight later, passing under the new concrete bridge.

Locomotive Class 56 *Bardon Mill* stationary on Windsor Road Bridge while permanent way maintenance work is carried out, August 1996.

Two class 37 locomotives assist at the rear of a special rail tour train en route for Boulby Potash mine, August 1990.

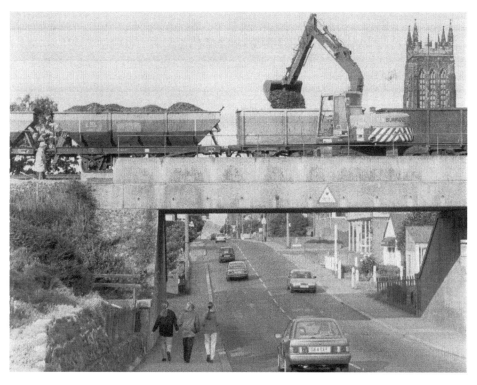

Maintenance work underway on Windsor Road railway bridge, 1993.

Above: North Eastern Railway Class P3 with a goods train approaching Saltburn near Tofts Crossing. Emmanuel church can be seen on the far right of this photograph taken by Frank Bainbridge.

Left: One of the 'Milestone sculptures' on Huntcliff frames a Class 37 locomotive as it passes with a loaded train of potash from Boulby mine. The building behind the locomotive is the Guibel fan house which drew fresh air through Huntcliff mine.

Opposite above: Railway fireman John Bulmer visiting Saltburn station signal cabin. The number of signal operating levers is testimony to the extensive railway system in the centre of Saltburn.

Opposte below: A diesel multiple unit arriving in Saltburn station from Darlington. At the time semaphore signals were still in use, however engineering work was in progress to replace them with coloured lights, making the signal cabin in the background redundant.

LNER Class locomotive L1 returning light engine to Thornaby Shed after bringing in the evening parcels van to Saltburn. The parcels van returned to Darlington attached to regular passenger D.M.U.

An unusual sight in Saltburn station, a High Speed Train 125 visiting Saltburn with a Hertfordshire Railtours special train.

LNER Class K1 locomotive 2005 arrives in Saltburn station with a special train from Newcastle, Sunday 17 August 1986.

LNER Class K1 locomotive 2005 arrives in Saltburn station with a special train from Newcastle on Sunday 17 August 1986 and welcomed by a large crowd. Brian Harrington found a vantage point in Gresley Court flats to photograph the busy scene.

Brian Harrington photographed LNER Locomotive Class A3 4472 *Flying Scotsman* arriving in Saltburn station to a huge reception on Sunday 16 August 1987. The crowd-pulling popularity of this locomotive is very obvious in this picture.

Diesel Class 55 Deltic locomotive 55009, *Alycidon*, was attached to the rear of the train hauled by *Flying Scotsman* at Saltburn station on Sunday 16 August 1987. Strawberry teas were served in the attached coaches during the afternoon. The photograph is by Brian Harrington.

Above and below: Crowds flocked to see the *Flying Scotsman* and the *Alycidon* during their visit to Saltburn in August 1987 as these busy scenes in Dundas Street West testify.

Saltburn station. 'The Boulby Flyer' is being prepared for one of its four return trips to Boulby Potash mine. The locomotive is Class 47 47773 *Reservist*. The trips were organised by the Saltburn Line Users Group on Sunday August 13 1995 and were all fully booked.

Saltburn station LMS locomotive 8F 48151 visiting Saltburn during the weekend of 16 and 17 August 1997. Whilst visiting Saltburn the locomotive was featured in a BBC Open University programme.

six

People

Above: Town crier Sharon Tinkler on duty in Station Square during Victorian Week 1987. Sharon strolled around the streets announcing events, times and venues throughout the week.

Left: Alan and Jean Watson pose in Victorian dress outside Alexandra House on Britannia Terrace on Sunday 16 August 1987, the final day of Victorian Week.

Opposite above: A visit by a horse–drawn omnibus owned by Tim Jackson from Guisborough provides unusual transport on the top promenade for townspeople and visitors on Sunday 16 August 1987 during Victorian Week.

Opposite below: Traction engine *Lorna Doone*, driven by owner Tom Colledge, gave public rides during Victorian Week in August 1987.

Above: On a summer's day the ice cream seller does brisk business near the Cliff Lift during Victorian Week on Sunday 16 August 1987.

Left: Band concerts on the tea lawn near the Italian Gardens drew large crowds in Victorian Week and many dressed for the occasion. Bunty Newman is on the right-hand side of two visitors, with three of her grandchildren in front, August 1988.

Above: Part of a Victorian-dressed audience listening to a band concert on the tea lawn in the Valley Gardens in 1988. These were held as part of the August Victorian Week and were popular over many years.

Right: Strolling around the Italian Gardens in August 1988 while listening to the band playing on the nearby tea lawn, this group were suitably dressed in Victorian style to recall earlier days in the pleasure grounds. On the left are Kath Myers and Marjorie Duff.

People watching the town photograph being taken during Victorian Week. On this occasion the backdrop was Emmanuel church on Sunday 9 August 1992.

A family group taking afternoon tea in the Saltburn Community Centre hall during Victorian Week, August 1992.

Station Square was a focal point during Victorian Week; here we see Alan Waller conducting his band during a lunchtime concert. The open-top bus in the background toured the town with a jazz band playing on the upper deck, August 1993.

Above: Station Square was the setting for a display by the puppets of the 'Happy Wanderers' from Stockton. Cyril Hay is operating a beautifully dressed puppet which entrances the children in the audience in August 1993.

Opposite below: On the final Sunday of each Victorian Week a grand parade was held through part of the town, the final destination being the gathering for the town photograph which on this occasion, Sunday 8 August 1993, was Brockley Hall on Glenside. The three main figures are, from left to right, Abbi Worts, Yvonne Cooper and Rosemary Suscens.

Right: Traditionally a church service was held on the final Sunday of Victorian Week. A parade was formed at the station portico and made its way to the top promenade. Sandra Thomson and Michael Morrissey are seen here inviting members of the public to join in the parade and service on Sunday 15 August 1993.

Below: A Victorian Week open-air church service held near the top of the Cliff Lift on Sunday 15 August 1993.

Above: Many visitors attended the Victorian Week. This group, photographed in front of the Victoria Hotel in Dundas Street East, represented old time cyclists from Hull. They were met by the chairman of the parish council, David Jones, accompanied by his wife, on Thursday 9 August 1995.

Left: Competitions were held for the best-dressed families during Victorian Week. Olive Spoors from Garnet Street waits in Dundas Street near the Victoria Hotel for the judges' decision on Thursday 9 August 1995.

Opposite above: The Valley Gardens, originally named The Pleasure Grounds, with a Punch and Judy show giving pleasure to children in a performance on the tea lawn, Easter 1993.

Opposite below: On the site of the old potting sheds used by the resident gardeners in the Valley Gardens, a Woodland Centre was constructed. David Bellamy, the well-known botanist, accepted an invitation to open the centre and we see him getting down to the children's level, Sunday 16 October 1994.

A local army cadet unit provided marshals and assistance at entertainment in the Glen near to the Valley Gardens Woodland Centre at the opening day in 1994.

Three dancers taking part in the opening ceremony at the Woodland Centre in 1994. The temporary stage was erected near Skelton Beck in the Glen.

Saltburn Victorians are a group of enthusiasts dedicated to making and wearing authentic Victorian dress. They support events throughout the North of England. Here we see them waiting to greet passengers on a late-running Hertfordshire 125 Railtours excursion on Saturday 18 November 1989.

Children at Saltburn Infants School in Upleatham Street have a visit from the Saltburn Victorians on Monday 9 July 1990. It was part of a programme to introduce children to Saltburn's Victorian heritage.

Saltburn has been an entrant in Northumbria in Bloom and Britain in Bloom competitions for a number of years and a special welcome has always been made for the judges. In 1990 the judges were greeted by playgroup children at Northrifts, the home of Joan St Vaughan.

When the judges for Northumbria in Bloom visited Saltburn in 1991 they were treated to a ride on the Saltburn Miniature Railway through the Valley Gardens. Photographed with the locomotive *Prince Charles* are, from left to right: -?-, Lena Sanders, -?-, Eileen Robinson, Carole Miller, Veronica Boland, an In Bloom Judge, guard Ray Bowman, an In Bloom Judge, Geoff Briggs, and driver George Outhwaite.

Saltburn-by-the-Sea Women's Institute ladies are a very active group. They not only enjoy outings, meetings and craft events but also provide support for events in the town. On this occasion they provided lunch for the Northumbria in Bloom Judging visit on 15 April 2004. From left to right: Kath Glendenning, Olga Rylander, Barbara Matthews, Pauline Davies, Annette Lynch, Val Kerr, Eleanor Allanson, the two judges, Ruth Steere, Eileen Leonard, Cath Lynn, Ann Cowie.

Saltburn's Emmanuel church needs to raise funds and many events have been held throughout the years. On this occasion the Revd Marjorie Brookes helps out at the bric-a-brac stall.

Outdoor band concerts have been an important part of Saltburn's entertainment since the town was built. The loss of the bandstand in the Valley Gardens due to a direct hit by a German bomb in 1941 was finally remedied in 1997 when a new bandstand was opened on 24 July by the Mayor of Redcar and Cleveland Borough Council, Kath McBride.

At the opening of the new bandstand the townspeople were entertained by Marske brass band in the presence of the mayor of the borough, Kath McBride, and the chairman of the parish council, Alan Guy.

Right: Each Christmas a carol service is organised by the Saltburn Rotary Club. Accompanied by music from a brass band, carols are sung around the town's Christmas tree in Albion Terrace. Here we see children enjoying the event on a cold Sunday evening in 1988.

Below: Local businessman Don Hibbert was the mainstay of the Rotary Club carol service organisers for many years, and in all weathers. He is seen here leading the singing with members of the band on Sunday 19 December 1993.

Until the Second World War the Saltburn Fire Brigade was normally all retained firemen. They became full time, supported by auxiliary personnel. This group photograph taken in front of the fire station in Leven Street shows many of these personnel in around 1941. The boys in the front, who acted as messenger boys, are from left to right: Arthur Boyes, Norman Hudson, Eric Sibley, -?-. The officers in the centre of the second row are Mr Basil Metcalf, Mr Grant and Mr Bill Wardale. Second from the right in the back row is Mr Harrison.

Retained men in the Saltburn Fire Brigade provide an invaluable service to the town and surrounding area. They are seen here posing in front of the Dennis fire engine at the Leven Street fire station in Summer 1985. Left to right are Station Officer Michael Steere, Firemen Frank Copland, James Newcombe, Tommy Paterson, Walter Ross, Stanley Heward, Norman Glover, Ted Weatherill, Paul Thompson, Leading Fireman Bill Chapman, Fireman Clive Wilkinson, Leading Fireman John Murray, Firemen Brian Harrington and Eric Johnson.

Right: Retained firemen operate an output pump test at the Cat Nab car park with a Red Bedford water pump tender in the foreground and a red and silver Bedford water tender with a 60ft escape ladder. The fireman manning the water jet on the left-hand side is Michael Steere, with firemen Gordon Porter and Eric Johnson on the right-hand water hose, July 1969.

Below: Saltburn retained firemen organised a Christmas Toy Appeal. Toys were collected, broken toys were repaired and where necessary painted by the fire station personnel, and over 400 lots were collected between August and December 1987. Personnel included, from left to right: Station Officer Michael Steere, Leading Firemen Paul Thompson and Stanley Heward, Firemen Peter Jones, Martin Garret, Ted Weatherill, Chris Duncan, Chris Harrington and Eddie Guy.

An annual Carnival Week was held for a number of years. It encouraged many activities during the week and here we see radio-controlled model boats being demonstrated near Cat Nab car park.

Activities held in the Valley Gardens during Victorian Week included a duck race, organised on this occasion by the Redcar Lions Club. The crowd gathered at the finishing line near Cat Nab car park hoping to see their number on the first plastic duck to arrive. This bridge where the spectators are gathered was later washed away during a flood.

Open-air dancing on the top promenade to Alan Waller's dance band in August 1990. The music allowed people to demonstrate their dancing skills and entertain the public. The dance floor on this occasion was the paved area over the top of the water head tank for the water-balanced cliff lift.

A street entertainer involves children in his act in Station Square during Victorian Week, 1990. In the background is George Barnes with a video camera.

Street parties were held throughout the town during Victorian Week. Oxford Street residents provided a conjurer to entertain the children in 1990. Notice the look-alike Queen Victoria in the background.

Saltburn was home to a very popular Youth Hostel in Victoria Road. When it was threatened with closure in 1991 an open day was held and Richard Holt, who was a Member of Parliament at the time, opened the event and gave his support to the campaign to save the hostel from closure. Unfortunately the campaign was unsuccessful. Joan Sands is on the extreme left of the photograph and in the front row, forth and fifth from the left, are Harriet and Percy Ransom.

Evening classes were held in the local schools for furthering skills in various hobbies. This is the photographic class in around 1959. Back row, from left to right: -?-, Ken Bowers (tutor), Reg Blacklock, Roy Isles, David Simpson. Front row: Harry Brittain (tutor), George Medd, Walter Davidson.

Saltburn celebrated its centenary in 1961 and many events were held during this commemoration. A competition was held for the Centenary Princess and Pat Bowers was chosen, to be accompanied by Jill McEndo. Pat is here being presented with a crystal bowl by the chairman of the Saltburn and Marske Urban District Council, John Burns.

Opposite: Over the years there was much speculation over who was the first child to be born in Saltburn-by-the-Sea. Arthur Spencer's name was amongst those offered. In 1992 it was finally proved that Arthur Spencer was the first child born in the new town. Herbert Spencer Mabin, the maternal grandson of Arthur Spencer, was on holiday in the area from South Africa. We were contacted by him and able to take this photograph of him with a small bible, presented by the local registrar.

Right: Saltburn Halfpenny Bridge received this name because of the tolls paid by pedestrians crossing the bridge. The toll keeper collected the fee in a small building at the town side of the bridge. He is seen here with Mr Metcalfe the head gardener of the Valley Gardens. The bridge was owned by Skelton & Gilling Estates.

Below: Pitchforth the photographer captured many aspects of Saltburn both social and topographical. This photograph was taken on the wedding day of Robert Davies and Lucy Alexandra Pickles-Whiteley, outside No. 5 Zetland Terrace.

Above: Local businessman Cyril Pickering was master of the Cleveland Hunt. Meets were held nearby and in the town. On this occasion, in around 1958, the meet was held at the Ship Inn prior to moving into nearby Little Dale for the hunt. The ex-army wagon near to the Ship Inn was used for deliveries by A. Woodrow & Sons, coal merchants.

Above: Saltburn military band was formed from ex-members of the Church Lads Brigade. They were photographed on this occasion outside the Saltburn Cricket Club pavilion, *c.* 1909. The bandsman second from the left in the front row, is Arthur Ridley Garnett. Many of these bandsmen lost their lives in the First World War.

Right: During August 1992, Saltburn Valley Gardens was the venue for several performances of 'Pirates in the Park'. The events were a sell out and very well received. Stewards for the event were volunteers dressed for the occasion. Bunty Newman is in the centre of the trio.

Opposite below: Band concerts held in the bandstand on Glenside always attract large audiences, as witnessed on this sunny Sunday afternoon in 1997. The photograph was taken from the top of the tower of the Towers Building.

Phillip Chisholm and his daughter greet a very young motorist with music at the annual pre-Christmas event to celebrate the switching on of the town Christmas lights in Station Square on Friday 27 November 1992.

Saltburn Library is a focal point for many of the town's activities. In August 1996 there was a photographic exhibition illustrating the development of Saltburn and a chess afternoon was held. John Suscens seen here encourages a young player, Benjamen Hall.

The poultry farm on Marske Road began its existence on the site of an old isolation hospital. The site grew gradually from smallholding to farm and for many years was run by Tom Gladders and his wife Elsie. When they retired a farm sale was held and people are seen here viewing the lots for the sale on 29 May 1998.

Interest is being shown in some small sale items by the auctioneer and in the foreground a faithful old Ferguson tractor awaits its place in the selling programme. Tom and Elsie retired and went to live in Pickering.

During the First World War, Saltburn was virtually a garrison town. One unit billeted here was a battalion of the Welsh Regiment seen parading along Windsor Road to a drum head service in the grounds of the Girls High School on Marske Road.

When the Second World War broke out Saltburn once again became populated by military units. The Royal Army Ordnance Corps had their headquarters in Brockley Hall. Members of the unit pose together with ATS personnel on the former tennis courts on Windsor Road used by the Towers School. The present library was built on this site. In the second row from the front, fourth from the right, is Captain Ferguson and second from the right is Sergeant Freddy Wood.

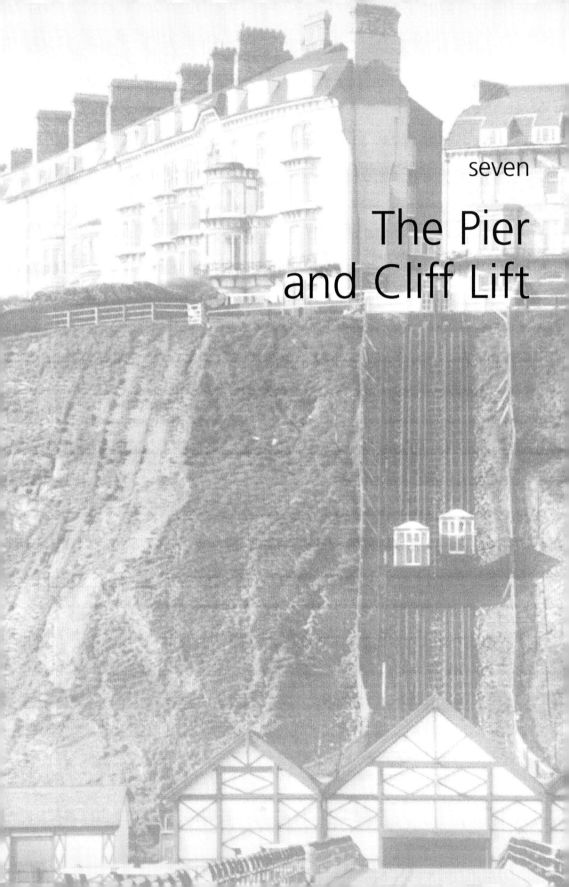

seven

The Pier
and Cliff Lift

In October 1867 a meeting was held in the Alexandra Hotel to form the Saltburn-by-the-Sea Pier Company Limited whose purpose was to erect and maintain a pier, extending 1,500ft into the sea and adapted as a promenade for landing passengers and goods from boats. It was also to construct a hoist for the conveyance of people to and from the beach to the level of the town. This photograph, taken in around 1869, shows work being carried out on the landing stage.

The pier was completed within seventeen months of the first pile being driven by Mrs Thomas Vaughan on 26 January 1868. It was opened to the public in May 1869. The pier company wound up its affairs in 1879 and the pier and hoist were sold by auction for £800 to the Saltburn Improvement Company. The landing stage was later washed away by storms and the pier was shortened. Shelters and a bandstand were provided at the seaward end. The small octagonal buildings were replaced by a small theatre and refreshment and retiring rooms at the shore end. This photograph is from around 1889.

In 1925 a larger theatre was built and a café provided at the shore end. The new theatre enabled a much wider range of entertainment to be provided and a café with delightful views catering for the visitors. The date of this photograph is around 1935.

Many incidents have threatened the existence of the pier over the years but it has survived and this photograph taken in September 2002 shows its excellent present condition after a thorough refurbishment. Grants from the National Lottery, European Community funding, Redcar and Cleveland Borough Council and Friends of Saltburn Pier have all contributed to its survival.

The sailing ship *Ovenbeg* was driven ashore onto the Marske side of the pier in May 1924. As the storm abated it appeared that the pier had escaped serious damage but the gales resumed and the ship was blown through the pier making it a total wreck. Several onlookers had to run for their lives. Frank Bainbridge managed to take this photograph just before the ship struck and then fled for the shore.

This gap caused by the wreck of the *Ovenbeg* was not repaired until 1934 when mild steel from Skinningrove ironworks was used in the repair. This photograph is from around 1925.

Musical entertainment in the pier bandstand was widely advertised, together with concerts in the Valley Gardens, inviting visitors on railway excursions to hear the music. The shelters on the pier provided a refuge from winds blowing from any direction.

The pier head in around 1963. The pier was closed to the public in 1973 and the pier head lost in a storm in 1974. Threat of total demolition hung over the whole structure but public campaigns led to a public enquiry in November 1975. As a result the pier was saved but with a much shorter length of 621ft 8in.

The pier seen from the cliff-top footpath in 1957 was an impressive sight. The section replaced after the *Ovenbeg* incident can clearly be seen in this photograph. Note the chalets to the Huntcliff side of Old Saltburn.

Looking towards Huntcliff from above Hazelgrove the 1,250ft length can clearly be seen, *c.* 1961. The chalets on the lower promenade are clearly visible.

Above: Following a Lottery funding award of £999,500, work commenced in May 2000 to renovate the pier section by section, with new supporting piles. The surprise to us all was the shallow depth of the Victorian piles into the sand and underlying shale bed. We could only marvel that the structure had survived so many storms over the years. Workmen are seen placing a prefabricated section of decking in position in 2000.

Right: Refurbishment work was carried out when tidal conditions allowed the heavy machinery to venture onto the sands. Great care was taken to ensure that the new piles aligned with the Victorian trestles. Work was carried throughout the night at times.

Before the Second World War the resident coastguards held an annual memorial service for people lost at sea, culminating in the casting of a poppy wreath onto the water. The Friends of Saltburn Pier revived this practice on three occasions during their fund-raising. Seen in the photograph are, from left to right: Tom Gladders, who took the service; Captain Jim Elliott; Norman Bainbridge, Chairman of the Friends of Saltburn Pier; Marjorie Bainbridge, Secretary of the Friends of Saltburn Pier; Peter Nixon; -?-; Alan Guy, Chairman of the Parish Council.

Attending the pier-end service in 1997 were representatives from the National Coast Watch and the RNLI. Captain Jim Elliott is third from left, Brian Wilkinson eighth from left and on the extreme right is Margaret Wilkinson.

Following renovation work on the pier an official reopening was held on Friday 13 July 2001.
Chris Smith MP made the opening speech and cut the ribbon. In the photograph are, from the
left, Ashok Kumar MP; Vilma Collins; Jackie Taylor; Brian Maidens; Tim Mickleburgh, Chairman
National Piers Society; Frank Bradley.

Children from Saltburn Primary School accompanied by their parents await the re-opening of
the pier.

Friends of Saltburn Pier provided two seats for the pier, which were installed in September 2003. Some of the Friends tested the seats. Seated are Marjorie Bainbridge, Joan Ford, Joan Guy and Joan Wells. Standing: Norman Bainbridge, Peter Ainsley, Fred Robinson,-?-, Mary Collins, -?-, Jack Barwick, John Wells, Frank Leng and Peter Nixon.

The view from the cliff lift as it descends towards the pier in 1986.

A vertical hoist designed by John Anderson, the engineer for the Saltburn Improvement Company, was erected in 1870 and opened to the public on 1 July 1870. It was of wooden construction with a single cage capable of carrying twenty people. It worked for thirteen years without an accident but was then declared unsafe and demolished.

The vertical hoist was quickly replaced by a water-balanced cliff lift opened for public use on 2 July 1884. The lift is now the oldest operating water-balanced cliff lift in the country. This view is from around 1888.

Left: The cliff lift in operation as seen from the pier. The carriages now carry twelve passengers and the journey time is twenty seconds. Water is added to the upper car until there is sufficient weight to raise the lower car. The speed of the cars is controlled by a braking system operated from the top cabin. In 1954 the charge was 2d to travel up and 1d to travel down.

Below: Maintenance work is constantly being carried out on the cliff lift to ensure the safety of the system. On 12 January 2000 both cars were removed for extensive renovation work. One car here is safely on a transport lorry while the other is being lifted over the buildings.

Right: After many years as the engineer in charge of the cliff lift, Ken Fellowes (centre) retired, in early 2005. Regular users of the lift presented Ken with a painting by local artist Pauline Hewitt. On his left is Alan Ismay, who is now engineer in charge, and Norah Peel, who works in the lower building taking the money.

Below: In the 1940s a young trainee engineer with the Saltburn and Marske Urban District Council drew a colourful, imaginary representation of how the lift works. The original drawing is on display in the lower entrance.

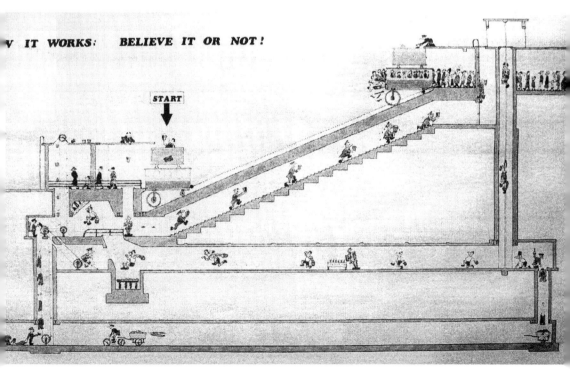

V IT WORKS: BELIEVE IT OR NOT!

START

The cliff lift has an excellent safety record but it is prudent to be prepared for any eventuality. Here are Saltburn retained firemen practising a rescue from the cars in mid-position.

The mock rescue was brought to a successful conclusion.

eight

By the Sea

Angling has always been popular from Saltburn Pier. Youngsters were encouraged to join the Junior Fishing Club and competitions were held with trophies awarded to the successful. In 1969 Mrs Ascough presented a winner's trophy. Vera Robinson, to her left, was the driving force behind the Junior Fishing Club.

The former bandstand at the pier head acted as the clubhouse for the Junior Fishing Club, c. 1936.

David Marshall of Middlesbrough takes part in a fishing competition for minors organised by the British Rail Social Section of Thornaby Motive Power Depot, in 1967.

Above: Sandcastle building and sand designs have always been a popular pastime on the beach. At times in the past competitions have been sponsored by national companies. In this photograph taken in 1902 the competition was sponsored by Bovril.

Left: Sponsored by an arts grant, Loui Robinson, with the help of children, created this sand sculpture of a sea horse. This viewpoint from the pier captures the scale of the sculpture. It was of course only a short-lived piece of work because it was soon enveloped by the incoming tide.

Right: Sea coal washed up on the beach provided a welcome source of fuel for many grates in the town, *c.* 1939. Gathering and transporting required a lot of effort to bring the spoils to the hearth. The gatherers on this occasion were, from left to right, Michael Pullean, John James Wilson, Arthur Elwood and Harry Vayro.

Below: John James Wilson, then aged around seventy years, transporting bags of sea coal from the beach to the promenade on his trusty old bicycle, *c.* 1939. When the sea coal arrived at its destination it was usually packed into small cone-shaped bags made from newspaper before being burnt on the fire.

Pony and donkey rides were one of the pleasures of being at the seaside. Jane Lynn held by her mother Cathleen appears to be enjoying the experience of this pony ride on a very busy day on the beach, *c.* 1960.

Right: A donkey is the chosen ride for Paul Bulmer who looks a little unsure whilst being held by his mother Joan. The donkeys and ponies were well looked after with regular breaks and feeds.

Opposite above: Plunging into the cold North Sea for charity in mid-winter is still a well-supported activity. Stewart MacFarlane does the final countdown for these hardy folk, some in fancy dress, on Boxing Day in 1989.

Opposite below: The race to the sea is on, lead by Stewart MacFarlane. Plenty of well wrapped-up spectators encourage the hardy folk but none lingered long in the sea on this cold Boxing Day in 1989.

Above: The end of the pier was very crowded when judging took place for the Saltburn Pier Queen in 1954. Sally Annear, second from the left, was the winner.

Left: Sally Annear, winner of the 1954 Saltburn Pier Queen competition, poses again for a photograph on National Piers Day, 30 June 1996. Now Mrs Sally Dixon, she holds the photograph taken on the day she won the title.

Above: Bathing machines were introduced on the beach at Saltburn in 1865. Bathers climbed on board while the machine was on dry sand and, as they were changing, a horse pulled the machine into the sea where the occupant was able to emerge in a bathing costume for a swim. The process was reversed after the swim. The old bathing machines were later used as day chalets near the Ship Inn.

Right: Sand yacht racing was a popular sport on the beach in the early 1900s. This photograph shows a fine example of a DIY sand yacht.

Following a display by the local lifeboats on Sunday 17 August 1986 the crowds begin to return to the town up the steep paths between the upper and lower promenades.

During the early 1930s several blocks of day chalets were built on the lower promenade, these being at the foot of Hazelgrove. Although they survived the Second World War they succumbed to vandalism and neglect in the 1960s and all except the block at the bottom of Saltburn Bank were demolished. The remaining chalets are now Grade II-listed buildings.

Entertainment was provided on the lower promenade during the summer months by troupes using a special small stage overhanging the beach. This photograph taken in 1935 is from the Jack Wright collection and shows the energetic entertainment being provided by the Jovial Jollies. A very low tide has left the beach covered with seaweed and the pier almost high and dry. The structural steel support for the stage was washed away during storms in early 1953.

Mrs Bert Grapho's Jovial Jollies pose on stage at the lower promenade venue showing the type of costumes worn. The photograph shows the restricted stage for the performance. This was typical seaside entertainment in the 1930s. Payment depended on the generosity of the audience as collections were taken after each show.

Entertainment for holidaymakers and townspeople was also provided by travelling fairs. On this occasion in 1935 it was on the ground behind Cat Nab. The kiddies' ride in the foreground provided a safe, gentle ride on vehicles representing then current transport models. In the background are the ever-popular Waltzers. This photograph is from the Jack Wright collection.

On occasions a stage was erected in the central shelter of the lower promenade to provide entertainment for visitors. In the foreground are Betty and Charles Humble, behind are Dave and Angela Gladders. The audience were enjoying a sponsored concert on National Piers Day, c. 1997.

An American Civil War re-enactment group visited Saltburn during Heritage Week in 1998 and fought a short battle on the beach near the pier. The main demonstration by the group took place in the Valley Gardens.

An appreciative audience watches the American Civil War re-enactment group perform during Victorian Week, 1998.

Above: The beach, although cleaned regularly by the Borough Council, still shows evidence of modern litter problems. Twice a year a survey initiated by the Marine Conservation Society under the title 'Adopt a Beach Scheme', is mounted by local volunteers. Ready to begin the survey in 2000 are, from left, Barry and Elsie Fish and Joan Guy, chairman of the parish council. Eighth from left is Miranda Kelly, and seated is Jackie Taylor, ready to record information.

Left: A team of Adopt a Beach volunteers show off some of the items recovered from the high-water mark – Dr Bill and Miranda Kelly with a young volunteer.

Above: Being 'by the sea' for most visitors from Victorian times until the late 1950s meant travel by rail to get there. There was a dramatic change when the motorcar became available to the masses, as can be seen from this photograph of a very busy Cat Nab car park in the late 1960s. A weir across the beck allowed safe boating.

Right: 'By the sea' to many people was a walk across the boards on a pier over the sea. It was popular in the Victorian era but is still so today as shown by this photograph taken on 18 July 2004.

Left: 'By the sea' in Victorian times had healthy associations - a dip in the sea was thought to be 'good for the well-being of people'. Today riding on the waves is the attraction. It began in the mid–1960s and is still extremely popular. These surfers were entering the sea at Saltburn on Saturday 25 March 2006.

Below: 'By the sea' thoughts bring back happy memories of childhood for most of us; freedom, building sandcastles, 'splodging in the sea' while parents relax, keeping an eye on their offspring. The windbreak is at times a very essential accessory.

'By the sea' was a time for watching the ships sail past, and from Victorian times to the 1920s this included sailing ships and steam-driven vessels. The sight of the Scottish herring fishing fleet off the coast at night was very special. Modern ships vary in size but *Queen Mary II* sailing past on 12 July 2004 attracted large crowds to top promenade. Sir Jimmy Saville, who in his younger days spent holidays in Teddy's Nook, had been influential in persuading Cunard to sail the ship close to the Yorkshire coast.

'By the sea' was also the vision of Henry Pease (1807-1881) who succeeded with his Saltburn Improvement Company in bringing a vision to reality and creating a firm foundation for the town we know today. His links with the Stockton & Darlington Railway Company brought the railway to the new town in 1861 and the building of the impressive Zetland Hotel is also credited to his influence. The controversial modern statue situated in the Rose Gardens opposite the convalescent home is now the only reference to him in the town.

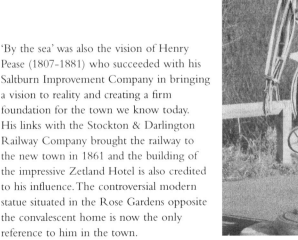

Other local titles published by The History Press

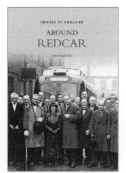

Around Redcar

SHEILA BARKER

This selection of over 220 old photographs illustrates some of the changes and events that have taken place in and around Redcar over the last century. The book also includes old images from the neighbouring communities of Coatham and Warrenby and recalls the life and times of local people at work and play throughout the area.

0 7524 3704 6

Around Grangetown

JOHN O'NEILL

Illustrated with over 200 images, this volume features some of the important events and developments that have taken place in this industrial town from the Victorian age through to the 1950s. It describes the impact of the iron and steelworks, which brought housing and employment to the area, and the effects of war on the community, as well as providing a unique pictorial history of aspects of everyday life, from schools and churches, pubs, shops and streets.

0 7524 3282 6

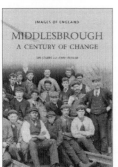

Middlesbrough A Century of Change

IAN STUBBS AND JENNY PARKER

Middlesbrough grew up entirely as a Victorian enterprise around the new industries of iron making, shipbuilding and, later, chemicals, along the banks of the Tees during the nineteenth century. This splendid selection of over 270 old photographs of Middlesbrough illustrates some of the many changes that occurred in the town over the twentieth century. These nostalgic images show the town and its buildings over the years and the people in factories, schools and at leisure, playing sport or watching celebratory events. The compilers of the book are both professionals in Middlesbrough's libraries and museums service.

0 7524 3720 8

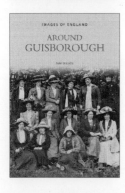

Around Guisborough

PAM WILSON

This collection of over 200 archive photographs portrays life in and around the town of Guisborough during the last 150 years. From snapshots of horse-drawn vehicles and charabancs, annual carnivals and motorbike gymkhanas, to views of children playing in fields which now house new generations of Gisborians, each picture reveals a gradual change in the buildings and streets and offers a unique glimpse into Guisborough's past.

0 7524 3075 0

If you are interested in purchasing other books published by The History Press, or in case you have difficulty finding any of our books in your local bookshop, you can also place orders directly through our website

www.thehistorypress.co.uk